I0158238

Bible Studies for Belts:
A Guide for Christian Martial Arts
Vol. 1: White Belt

By: John Blackman

ALL RIGHTS RESERVED. NO PART OF THIS PUBLICATION
MAY BE REPRODUCED IN ANY FORM OR BY ANY MEANS,
INCLUDING SCANNING, PHOTOCOPYING, OR OTHERWISE
WITHOUT PRIOR WRITTEN PERMISSION
OF THE COPYRIGHT HOLDER.

COPYRIGHT © 2016 AMERICAN
CHRISTIAN DEFENSE ALLIANCE, INC.
Baltimore, Maryland

ACDAINC.ORG

Special Request

Thank you for purchasing our book and supporting our Ministry. We have a Special Request for those that have purchased this book on the Kindle platform. We wanted to make you aware that Amazon's Kindle platform pays per pages "read". Our Special Request is that if you appreciate our Ministry's efforts to put out books such as this or if you would simply like to support our Ministry's work to please scroll to the back of the book, even if you don't "read" the book right away. This is how we will get paid through the paid per pages criteria.

We all lead such busy lives nowadays and can get side tracked so easily please take a moment to support us now by allowing us to be paid by scrolling to the end of the book – Then go back and read it at your leisure. Also don't forget to get your print copy of the book today and take it with you on the go.

We deeply appreciate Your support and know that God will Bless You as You have Blessed this Ministry.

Dedication

This Book is dedicated to the Lord Jesus Christ who gave Himself freely that everyone could have the opportunity to be free in Him and enter into the Kingdom of Heaven.

This book is also dedicated to every Christian Martial Arts practitioner out there who seeks to serve the Lord Jesus Christ with a pure heart and a sincere conscious as well as those around them to the fullest of their abilities.

~Faith, Family, and Freedom~

<u>Core Pillars</u>

Acknowledgment

I'd like to acknowledge Sensei Josh Velasquez as the individual who presented the concept of Defending Your Faith to the American Christian Defense Alliance Martial Arts Ministry. Sensei Velasquez has been part of the American Christian Defense Alliance Martial Arts Ministry for a number of years now. He is been certified through the American Christian Defense Alliance and currently holds the position of Virginia State Representative within the American Christian Defense Alliance.

Our organization worked with Sensei Velasquez and encouraged him to develop Seisho Ryu Karate as an extension of our Martial Arts Ministry Seisho Ryu Ninjutsu. The American Christian Defense Alliance recognizes Josh Velasquez as the founder of Seisho Ryu Karate and has awarded him certification as such.

Sensei Josh Velasquez runs the Harvest Martial Arts Academy in Chesapeake, Virginia at One City Church.

For more information regarding Sensei Josh Velasquez or his Ministry please check our website at www.acdainc.org

If you contact Sensei Josh Velasquez with the information I have provided in this book please let them know where you found his information.

Forward

First off I would like to congratulate you for purchasing this book, "Bible Studies for Belts: A Christian Martial Art's Guide Vol. 1: White Belt". We deeply appreciate your purchase and hope that you enjoy this book.

The purpose of this book is to assist those within the American Christian Defense Alliance, Inc. Martial Arts Ministry with a resource to help them better understand the operational framework of the Biblical aspects of our Martial Arts Ministry system and style.

In this book we hope to create unity throughout the Christian Martial Arts world by establishing a set standard to utilize while discipling students in the faith.

The ultimate goal for any Christian Martial Arts Ministry should be to disciple brothers and sisters in the Lord. There is such an attack on the fundamental principles of the Word of God in this current time that it's clear to see if we don't do something then we will lose everything.

Jesus last Commandment was to go and make disciples throughout all of the world. He knew that there was coming a time and day when believers would not walk in sound doctrine. This is why He continually emphasized that we should watch and pray lest anyone deceive us.

There is no greater thing that we can do to help change the situations around us that we find less then desirable than to love those around us and make disciples as the Lord commanded us.

Some may be asking, how do you make disciples? Well the simple fact is we do have an example in Christ. He spent over three years with His disciples, they ate, slept, traveled, and all work together to support the ministry over that time.

The reality is discipleship is a complete immersion into a way of life, in this case the Christian way of life. Martial Arts is merely a tool to enable us to reach those interested in self-defense. We hope that you will join with us and use this book as a reference guide to discipling believers in the faith. If you are part of the American Christian Defense Alliance Martial Arts Ministry in some way this book is a must have for your Ministry

The operational framework of the Biblical concepts and aspects of our Martial Arts Ministry includes a multilayered system approach.

Specifically we use a three-tiered system which incorporates what we call, "Colors of the Cross" "Learning through Creation" and "Defending Your Faith". The three-tiered system approach works in harmony together to help solidify a solid operational framework of Biblical principles covered for each belt level.

Table of Contents

Chapter 1: How to utilize this Book

First and foremost it's important to understand how to best utilize this book and study each chapter to take full advantage of the knowledge and material contained in it.

The number one thing before starting any study on the Word of God is to pray and ask God to lead you and to guide you as you read the material contained in the study.

God says knock and the door will be open (Rev. 3:20) If your motives are pure, your heart sincere, and you diligently seek Him and His righteousness first, all things will be added on to you according to His will. Just understand it is through the Spirit of God in which you will be taught all things that you need to know according to God's time not ours.

In this book you will have three distinct areas to study. It's important to study them individually and separately. Once you have went through them individually your next step would be to combine all of the elements together to gain a more dynamic understanding of the message that's trying to be conveyed.

Why do we have a seven belts you might ask - this is not traditional. You are absolutely correct that this is not a traditional organizational flow. There are seven different belt levels, but you start with no belt as a level.

There are seven belt levels to represent the seven Days of Creation as written in the Holy Bible. Each different belt level represents an attitude if you would of each day of creation. Furthermore, each belt level also incorporates a specific Biblical teaching regarding the principles behind that day as well as the color of the belt level.

Chapter 2: Is it Biblical?

Often time people's view of Christians are as timid and defenseless. A Christian would never exhibit physical aggression, would they?

The Bible tells us in the book of Ecclesiastes that there is a time for everything . . . . . .

To every thing there is a season, and a time to every purpose under the heaven: A time to love, and a time to hate; a time of war, and a time of peace. ~Ecclesiastes 3:1, 8

So often in today's politically correct charged atmosphere Christians are being labeled in various ways to marginalize them, oppress them, and ultimately kill them as written in Matthew 24. The Bible declares very clearly that we will be hated in all the world for Christ namesake. It's important to understand this reality and the reality that we are in a spiritual war that has eternal consequences when studying this book.

Chapter 3: The White Belt

White Belt is the first belt that you will earn in our Christian Martial Arts Ministry system. You accomplish this through mastery of the fundamental principles and aspects that make up the foundation of our Martial Arts Ministry system.

In our Christian Martial Arts System we help to build your character through the Word of God in what we call "Operational Training". Part of this training includes this Bible Study series to give you the knowledge of the truth in a manner in which you have practical application in your everyday life. Our physical teachings we call, "Applied Technical Training" for those wondering.

Remember 2 Cor. 4:7-10

Chapter 4: Colors of the Cross - White –Focus is on Holiness

For us white represents holiness, light, purity, righteousness – it is the beginning stages of becoming sanctified onto the Lord. It is also the color that sets the stage for creating something new, as in a blank canvas.

Teaching on the color White – Focus on Holiness Continued . . .

White represents the light of awareness leading to perfection in Christ. The objective for the new student in our system is to shine the light into the darkness through persevering and enduring while training, to know good from evil, and to divide the word of God properly.

As God so-called light into existence you also simply believe – meaning no hesitation, no mental, emotional, physical, or spiritual walls up – just accept and do at this point in your training without questioning. Now this is more so referring to our physical training but it does have implications into the Biblical study here at white belt for you are either going to believe the Word of God as absolute truth or you're not – and that is our starting point.

Questions for Students:

Questions about the Word of God

1. What is Scripture? Heb. 4:12
2. What does the Scriptures Do? Heb. 4:12
3. Who is the Word of God?
4. What does 2 Tim 2:15
5. How shall we live? Matt. 4:4 / Luke 4:4
6. What is the Word of God called in Luke 8:11

7. Who is your family? Luke 11:28
8. Who hears God's Word? John 8:47
9. Who speaks the Word of God? John 3:34
10. How does Faith come? Rom 10:17
11. Is the Word of God chained? 2 Tim 2:9
12. Can the Word of God sanctify? 1 Tim 4:5
13. What does 1 Thess. 2:13 Say?
14. What is the Word of God called in Eph. 6:17?
15. Write Out 2 Cor. 2:17.
16. What happens if you keep God's Word? 1 John 2:5
17. We are strong because? 1 John 2:14
18. What did the souls get slayed for in Rev. 6:8?
19. Who reigns with Christ in Rev. 20:4
20. What happens if we change or alter the Bible? Rev. 22:18-19

Questions about Holiness

1. How should we worship the Lord? 1 Chron. 16:29
2. What does Psalm 29:2 say?
3. You have fruit unto what? Rom 6:22
4. How do we perfect holiness? 2 Cor. 7:1
5. What are you supposed to put on? Eph. 4:24
6. What is our hearts established in? 1 Thess. 3:13
7. Write out 1 Thess. 4:7.

Questions about Light

1. What happened after Jesus was Baptized? Matt. 3:16
2. What sprung up? Matt. 4:16
3. Who is the light of the World? Matt. 5:14
4. Write out Matt. 5:16.
5. If God tells you something in the dark, what should you do? Matt. 10:27

6. Through the tender mercy of God what did He do? Luke 1:78-79
7. What do you need to take heed of in Luke 11:35-36?

Questions about the Sanctification

1. Why should we glory in the Lord according to 1 Cor. 1:29-31?
2. What is the will of God? 1 Thess. 4:3.
3. What is sanctified in 1 Peter 1:2
4. Why did Paul give thanks in 2 Thess. 2:13?
5. How should we possess our vessel? 1 Thess. 4:4
6. By His mercy through what are we saved? Titus 3:5
7. Write Rom. 12:2 in your journal.

John 8:12 - Then spake Jesus again unto
them, saying, I am the light of the world: he
that followeth me shall not walk in
darkness, but shall have the light of life.

Chapter 5:

Learning through Creation

In the beginning God created the heaven and the earth. And the earth was without form, and void; and darkness was upon the face of the deep. And the Spirit of God moved upon the face of the waters. And God said, Let there be light: and there was light. And God saw the light, that it was good: and God divided the light from the darkness. And God called the light Day, and the darkness he called Night. And the evening and the morning were the first day. ~Genesis 1:1-5

Teaching on Day of Creation

Just like God's universe had a beginning, you have a beginning in the world of martial arts and in your Christian life in Christ.

You are starting fresh. You are at the beginning of your training just as when you were once newly born in Christ.

In order to earn your white belt you will need to master basic techniques, movements, and prove yourself to have obtained a specific level of physical fitness in addition to passing this study. In short, you need to be able to show and tell what you've learned.

Now let's compare that to growing in your relationship with God.

The first step in having a relationship with God is to believe God *is* and to want to get to know Him. Once you are there, you will need to get to know who God is, what His Word has to say, and to be able to tell anyone who asks (including yourself) *why* you want to be a Christian or why you believe what you believe.

1. What does Heb. 11:3 say?
2. What does 2 Peter 3:5 say?
3. What Avails in Gal. 6:15?
4. Write out John 1:1-5.
5. Who are the Sons of God in Rom 8:14?
6. What happens in 1 Cor. 6:11?
7. What does the Spirit search in 1 Cor. 2:10?

White Belt Learning through Creation
Scripture Memory Verse:

2 Cor. 5:17 - Therefore if any man be in Christ, he is a new creature: old things are passed away; behold, all things are become new.

Chapter 6:

Defending Your Faith

In this section of Bible Studies for Belts you are asked to defend your faith and answer various questions concerning your faith. If you're looking for certification after completing this study through the American Christian Defense Alliance Martial Arts Ministry then you will need to record your response in 720p or 1080p and upload your video to YouTube. Remember all certification come directly from us – Contact us for details on our website listed in this book.

Teaching on White Belt Topic

In this section you will find scriptural references from the Word of God pertaining directly to the white belt questions asked in the Defending Your Faith section of this study.

Scripture to Study

1. Write out Rev. 12:11 in your journal.
2. Why will you be brought before governors and kings? Matt. 10:18
3. Are you prepared to deal with Mark 13:9?
4. What will happen in Luke 21:12-14?
5. What can you not see if you are not born again? John 3:3-5
6. Write out John 3:16-18
7. How are you Jesus disciple? John 8:31
8. Why has Jesus come? John 10:10
9. What do you need to please God? Heb. 11:6

10. What is Faith? Heb. 11:1-3
11. Add Your Scripture: _____
12. Add Your Scripture: _____

John 14:6 - Jesus said to him, "I am the way, the truth, and the life. No one comes to the Father except through Me.

- Do you believe in the Bible as the Absolute Truth and Word of God? If so why?

- Give your personal testimony and/or evidence presented in creation. An example of this would be the wind. You cannot see the wind but you can see the effects of the wind. You cannot see the wind but you can feel it on your face.

Chapter 7: Lesson Wrap-Up

Key Point of White Belt Study

God desires for you to be Holy, to renew your mind with His Word, and to seek sanctification by His Spirit. Through this you will gain the necessary level of awareness to give yourself a tactical edge against your sin nature and spiritual enemy (by not allowing open doors to the enemy).

Rom. 8:31 - What then shall we say to these things? If God is for us, who can be against us?

- John 8:12 - Then spake Jesus again unto them, saying, I am the light of the world: he that followeth me shall not walk in darkness, but shall have the light of life.

- John 14:6 - Jesus said to him, "I am the way, the truth, and the life. No one comes to the Father except through Me.

- 2 Cor. 5:17 - Therefore if any man be in Christ, he is a new creature: old things are passed away; behold, all things are become new.

Students Skills Section:

- Meditate on Key Points and Scripture Memory Verses

- Write a 200-500 Article on Your Take Away as a Student

Watch the following movies:

- End Game
- Invisible Empire
- Shadow Government
- Wake Up or Waco

Special Gift

There is no formal prayer of salvation as many churches would have you believe, God's Word is very clear - there is only one way to get to the Father in heaven and that is through Jesus Christ (John 14:6). Jesus says that you must be born again to enter into heaven (John 3:3-5).

Salvation is simply the first step in building an open and honest relationship with God. We all have sinned and fall short every day, but there is Hope in Jesus Christ - Just cry out to God in sincerity and honesty asking for forgiveness and for Him to Save you, Sanctify you, and fill you with His Holy Spirit - Ask for His will to be done in your life on earth as it is in Heaven and That's it, now just keep it real with God.

A Warning:

The Christian walk is not an easy life on the surface. The Word of God says that we will be hated in all the world for Christ namesake (Matt. 24:9). The Bible says that in the last days are enemy prevail against us physically until Christ returns to save us (Dan 7:21, 22). Furthermore, we must endure hardship as a good soldier of Jesus Christ (2 Tim 2:3) and yet we are never alone in this, God promises us that He will never leave us nor forsake us if we believe in him (Matt.28:20).

In everything we go through we have the peace and joy of God which surpasses all understanding (Philp. 4:6-8) The Bible declares, "For I consider the sufferings of this present time are not worthy to be compared with the glory which shall be revealed in us". (Rom 8:18). However, in all these things we are more than conquerors through Jesus Christ (Rom. 8:37)

Stay In Contact

Our Contact Information

Stay in Contact with the American Christian Defense Alliance, Inc.
Contactus@acdainc.org Or Email Us Though Our Website At: www.ACDAInc.Org

Join Our Mailing List

We also Greatly Appreciate You Signing Up For Our Mailing List and Providing a Good Rating and review for this Book. Your reviews help other people like yourself find this book on Amazon and benefit from its contents.

If You or Your Family have been Blessed by this book please let us know by dropping us a line through our website at http://acdainc.org

Thanks Again for Reading

God Bless!

Find All Our Books On Amazon

Our Books on Amazon:

Martial Arts Ministry: How To Start A Martial Arts Ministry

Dirt on Your Tabies: 7 Short Stories of Seisho Ryu Ninjutsu

Real Men Don't Make Promises: Understanding Oaths, Pacts, Covenants & Promises From A Biblical Perspective

A Vague Notion: How To Overcome Limiting Beliefs of Fear and Anxiety Through the Word of God

Biblical Bug Out: Don't Bug In - Follow The Calling

Christian Prepping 101: How To Start Prepping

Prepping: A Christian Perspective

Prepping: Survival Basics

Bug Out: Prepper Preparations for Survival, SHTF, Natural Disasters, Off Grid Living, Civil Unrest, and Martial Law to Help You Survive the End Times

Overcoming 50 Shades of Grey And All The Colors Of The LGBT Rainbow: How To Conquer Your Lust and Walk In The Spirit Of God

Salvation for Your Unsaved Mom: 10 Things to Tell Your Mom Before She Dies

The Perfection of Purity: A Message To My Daughter

How To Finance Your Full-Time RV Dream

www.ingramcontent.com/pod-product-compliance
Lightning Source LLC
Chambersburg PA
CBHW021922040426
42448CB00007B/870

* 9 7 8 1 9 4 4 3 2 1 3 1 4 *